My Signing Book of Numbers

Patricia Bellan Gillen

KENDALL GREEN PUBLICATIONS
Gallaudet University Press
Washington, D.C.

Kendall Green Publications
An imprint of Gallaudet University Press
Washington, DC 20002

Library of Congress Cataloging-in-Publication Data

Gillen, Patricia Bellan.
   My signing book of numbers / Patricia Bellan Gillen.
      p.   cm.
   Summary: Teaches in sign language the numbers 0-20, 30-100 by tens,
1,000 and 1,000,000.
   ISBN 0-930323-37-8
   1. Sign language—Juvenile literature. 2. Counting—Juvenile literature.
(1. Sign language. 2. Counting.) I. Title.
HV2476.G55 1988
419—dc19   87-28758
(E)   CIP
                                                                  AC

Gallaudet University is an equal opportunity employer/educational
institution. Programs and services offered by Gallaudet University receive
substantial financial support from the U.S. Department of Education.

For my husband Vince
and all of his colleagues
in the teaching profession

1 2 3 4 5
6 7 8 9 10

numbers

zero
eggs

one
elephant

two
trucks

three
kangaroos

four
clowns

5

five
tigers

six
robots

seven
umbrellas

eight
elves

nine squirrels

ten
shirts

eleven
turtles

twelve
hamburgers

thirteen
chickens

fourteen
butterflies

fifteen
pumpkins

sixteen
worms

seventeen
toothbrushes

eighteen

bananas

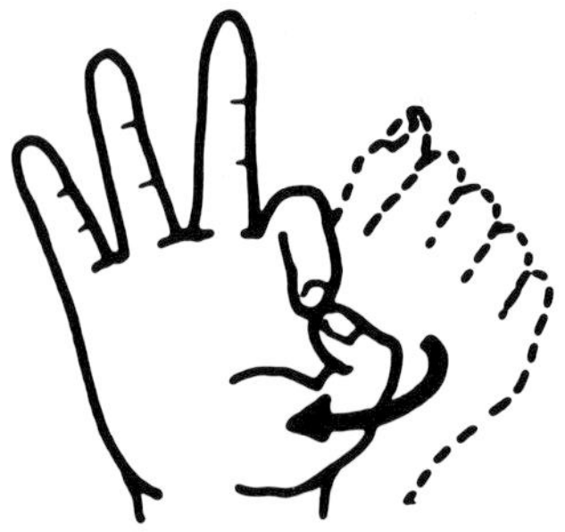

19

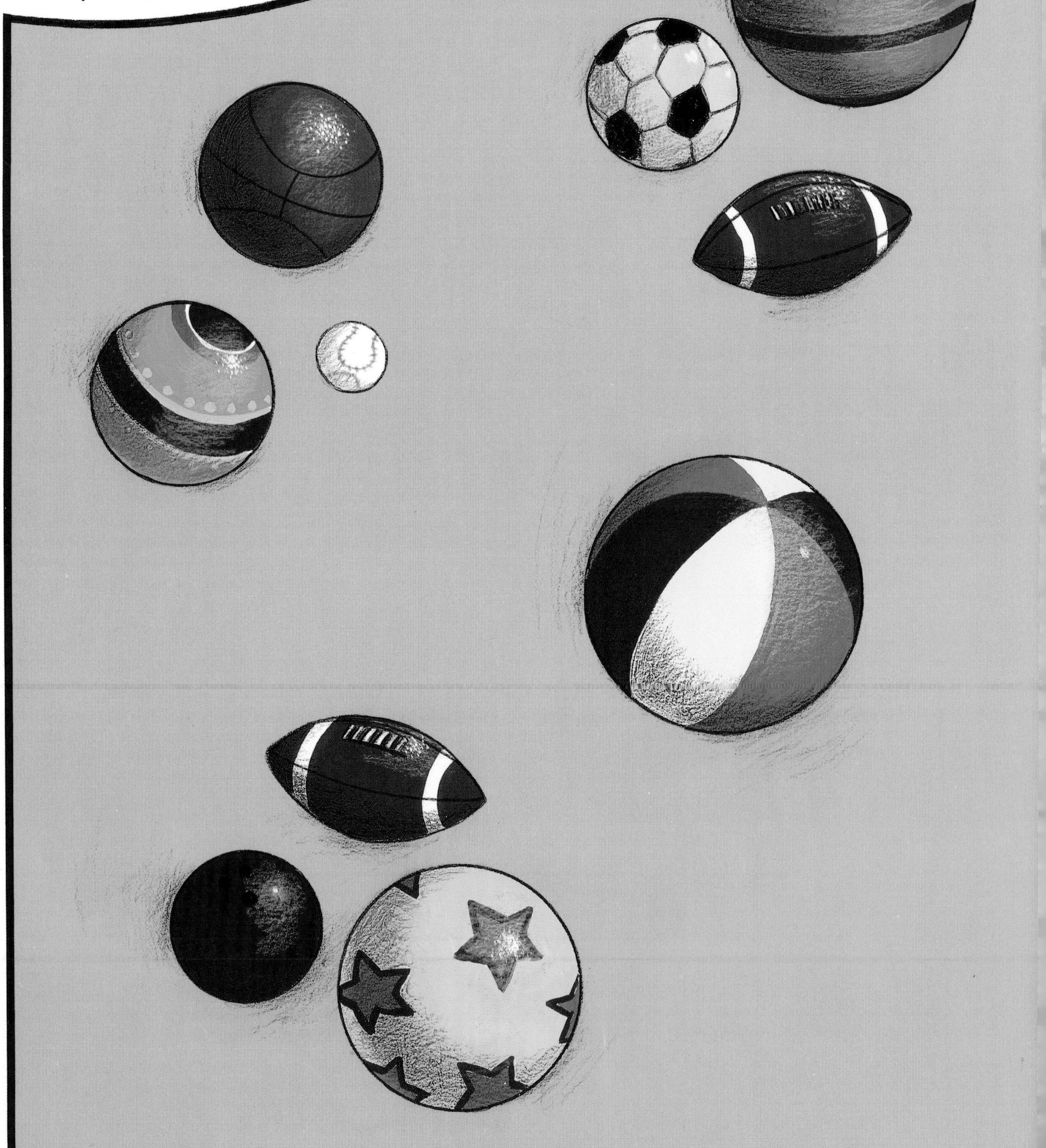

nineteen
balls

twenty
bugs

30

thirty
dollars

40

forty
pennies

50

fifty
mice

60

sixty
fish

70

seventy
hearts

80

eighty
triangles

90

ninety
circles

100

one hundred
squares

All About Signing Numbers

Children have a special fascination with sign language. They see signing on television, in the movies, and even in school. Children also have the ability to learn languages faster, and easier, than adults. *My Signing Book of Numbers* is for all children who have an interest in sign language.

As parents, one of the first things we teach our children when they begin to talk is the alphabet and the numbers *one* to *ten*. We all probably have childhood memories of singing the ABCs ourselves and of counting as we walked up and down the steps. We probably don't think of these abilities as more than rote repetition of children's songs and games, yet they are important skills in our early development. These skills are handed down from parent to child and are passed from generation to generation. Hearing-impaired children of hearing-impaired parents learn the alphabet and numbers in much the same way, only they repeat what they've learned *on their hands* instead of by talking. And they pass on these skills to their hearing friends.

About This Book

The purpose of this book is to show young children how to sign their numbers. American Sign Language has specific signs to represent all of the numbers. All the manual numbers can be made on one hand, making it practical as well as easy. With the basic handshapes for 0 through 15, all manual numbers can be signed. For example, 17 is a combination of the signs for 10 and 7; 45 is a combination of 4 and 5; and 1,362 is a combination of 1,000, 300, 6, and 2.

The objects represented in this book were chosen for various reasons. Some first appeared in *My First Book of Sign,* so they give a feeling of familiarity and continuity to children who have used that book. Many of the words are useful, everyday concepts that children encounter, like *eggs, balls, shirts, toothbrushes,* etc. Still other words were chosen because they have fun signs — *robots, bugs, kangaroos, turtles,* etc. These words also help to increase a young child's vocabulary.

My Signing Book of Numbers is not meant to

Manual Numbers

be a counting book; however, it can be used for this purpose if a child is old enough to understand this concept. Once a child can count, there are two more signs that may be helpful—*count* and *how many.*

count

Right hand F shape, left hand open; right palm down, left palm at an angle; move right thumb along left palm from heel to fingertips.

how many

Both hands open and curved; palms down; put hands in front of chest, index fingers touching, then roll fingers together until little fingers are touching and the palms are up. Then close fingertips, separate the hands and bring them straight up, opening the hands.

American Sign Language

American Sign Language (ASL) is recognized by many school systems as a legitimate language, like Spanish and French, and it is being taught as a language elective. Like these other languages, ASL has a grammatical base different from English and a vocabulary all its own. ASL has idioms and slang, and like other languages, slight nuances in a sign or the facial expression used with it can alter the meaning being conveyed.

ASL has three major components—signs, fingerspelling, and facial expressions.

Signs

The signs are the vocabulary of ASL. Each sign represents a specific concept; therefore, signs cannot be substituted for English words without considering the meaning implied in a specific context. For example, the English word *run* can have many different meanings. Similarly, the sign for *run* varies with its implied meaning in a specific sentence. In each of the following

sentences the meaning of *run* and the sign for *run* is different: He runs every morning before work; The senator is running for reelection; My nose is running; She runs a large company.

Each sign in ASL has three basic features: *handshape, position,* and *movement. Handshape* is usually a letter in the manual alphabet or a modification of a letter. The modified handshapes used in this book are shown in the chart on page 53. *Position* refers to the initial placement of the hands when beginning a sign. Almost all signs are made in the area between the forehead and the waist. The most comfortable position for signing, and the place easiest to see, is in front of the chest. At this level, people can see the hands and the mouth at the same time. *Movement* is where the hands move while making the sign. Movement can be up, down, away from the signer, toward the signer, etc. **All of the sign descriptions in this book follow this order: handshape—position—movement.**

Fingerspelling

Fingerspelling is a manual representation of the alphabet. Each letter is made with a specific handshape, and all the handshapes are made on one hand. When a sign doesn't exist for a particular English concept (for example, personal names, geographical locations, and newly created English words), the word is fingerspelled. When spelling a word, say the word being spelled instead of saying the individual letters.

The manual alphabet is easy to learn, and with it, children can and do carry on full conversations. Many children think of it as a secret language and use it in school, where they're not supposed to be talking.

Facial Expression

Facial expression is important in all forms of communication, but it is especially important in ASL. The meaning of a word or phrase can change depending on the signer's expression. For example, the intent of the word *angry* can range from mild annoyance to intense anger by how much the signer knits the eyebrows and clenches the teeth. Facial expressions present the most difficulty to beginning signers — it can be hard enough trying to remember where to put your hands. Just keep in mind that the quality of communication will be enhanced by the use of facial expressions with signing.

American Manual Alphabet

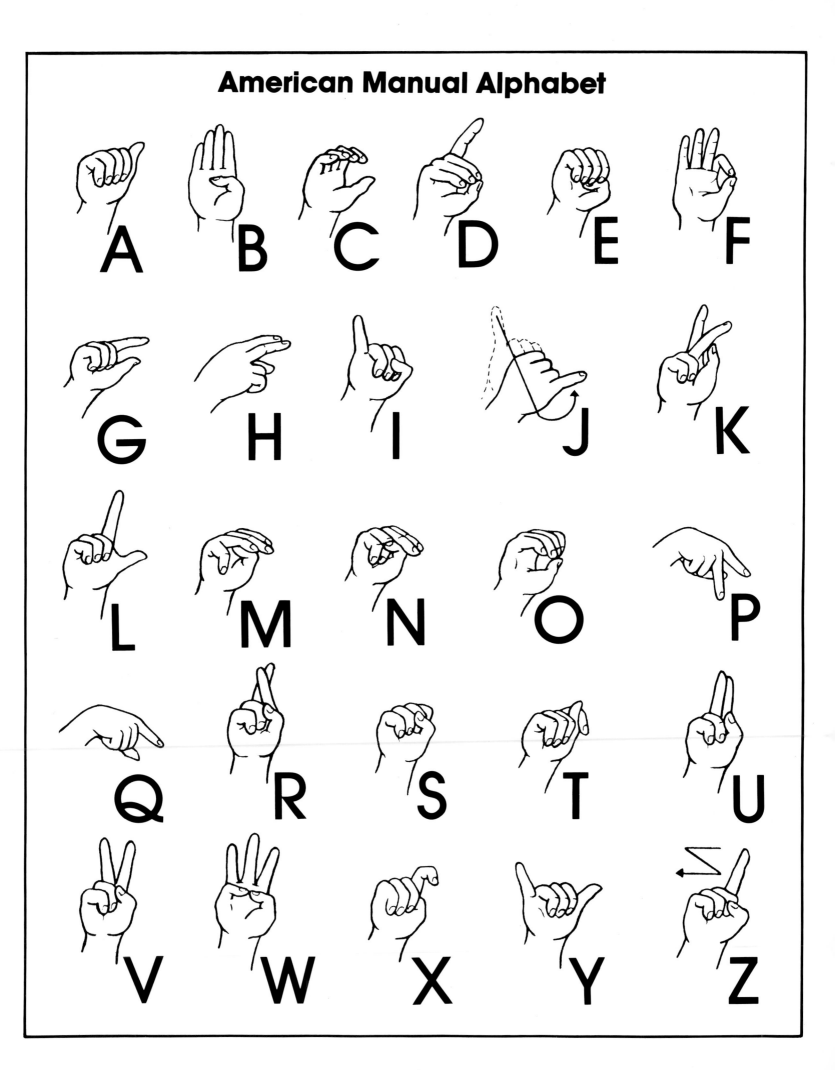

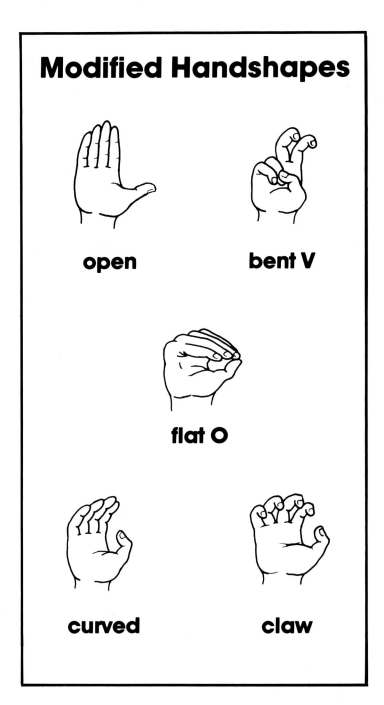

Modified Handshapes

open

bent V

flat O

curved

claw

Using This Book

The following section contains illustrations and descriptions of how to sign all the objects in this book. The arrows indicate the direction the hands move; a double-headed arrow means the hand moves in two different directions (either up and down, side to side, or in and out), and two arrows mean the same movement is repeated. The broken lines show the first position of the sign and the solid lines show the final position. All of the signs are drawn as they would look to the person reading the sign, not the signer. **And the sign description follows the order: handshape—position—movement.**

Many of the signs in ASL are made with two hands; however, one hand plays a dominant role in the sign. A signer's dominant hand is the hand used most often (right for right-handed people, left for left handers). Usually, one hand remains stationary, acting as a base or foundation, while the dominant hand moves. Some signs are made with both hands moving in symmetrical patterns, and other signs are made with only one (the dominant) hand. Similarly, the manual alphabet and numbers are signed by the dominant hand. The signs and numbers in this book are shown with a dominant right hand. Left-handed children and adults can just reverse the explanations and switch hands.

All of the objects represented in this book, except elephant, are plural. In ASL, the idea of plurality is usually conveyed by repeating the sign. Therefore, all the sign descriptions include a phrase such as, "and repeat," or "repeat the movement several times." The sign illustrations show how to sign the concept once.

Sign Descriptions

balls

Both hands C shape; palms facing; put hands in front of chest with thumbs and fingertips touching, then move hands apart and back together several times.

bananas

Left hand ONE shape, right hand flat O shape; left palm out, right palm left; hold left hand in front of chest and move right hand from top to base of left index finger several times while moving right hand around left index finger.

bugs

3 shape; palm left; place thumb on nose and bend index and middle fingers a few times.

butterflies

Both hands open and curved; both palms in; interlock thumbs and move fingers in and out repeatedly like wings flapping.

chickens

Thumb and index finger straight and touching, other fingers closed; palm facing out; place hand at side of mouth and open and close thumb and index finger several times.

circles

ONE shape; palm out; hold hand at chest level and draw a few circles in the air with the index finger.

clowns

C shape; palm in; place hand in front of nose and move hand in and out a few times.

dollars

Right hand curved, left hand open; right palm left, left palm in; grasp left fingers with right fingers and slide right hand off left fingertips; repeat.

eggs

Both hands H shape; right H across left H; place hands in front of chest and move hands down and apart; repeat.

elephant

C shape; palm out place hand at nose and then make a curve forward and down like an elephant's trunk.

elves

G shape; palms facing; place hands near ears and arc up while closing thumbs and index fingers; repeat.

fish

Both hands open; palms facing, fingers out; place left fingertips on heel of right palm, then wriggle right fingers and move hands forward.

hamburgers

Both hands open and curved; right palm down, left palm up; clasp palms together, right hand on top of left, then flip the hands and reverse the action; repeat.

hearts

Both hands 5 shape; palms in; bend middle fingers and trace the outline of a heart over the heart; repeat.

kangaroos

Both hands open and curved; both palms down; place right hand on back of left hand, and move hands forward in several bouncing motions.

leaves

Right hand 5 shape; left hand ONE shape; right palm in, fingers down, left palm in; place left index finger on palm side of right wrist and swing right hand back and forth several times

mice

ONE shape; palm left; place index finger on nose and brush across the nose several times.

number

Both hands O shape; palms facing; place fingertips of hands together, then twist hands back and forth a few times.

pennies

ONE shape; palm in; place index finger above right eye, then move hand out and back several times.

pumpkins

Right hand 8 shape, left hand S shape; both palms down; place right thumb on back of left hand and flick middle finger off the thumb several times.

robots

Both hands open; right palm left, left arm straight down; bend right arm at waist level, then lower right arm and raise left arm, bending at waist level and repeat both motions.

shirts

Thumb and index finger touching, other fingers closed; palm in; place right hand below right shoulder and grab shirt material between thumb and index finger.

squares

Both hands ONE shape; palms out; start with index fingertips touching, then trace a square in the air using both index fingers; repeat.

squirrels

Both hands bent V shape; palms facing; put hands in front of mouth with index and middle fingers touching, move fingers apart and back together several times.

stars

Both hands ONE shape; palms out; place index fingers side by side and alternately move fingers up and down.

tigers

Both hands claw shape; palms in; place hands at sides of mouth and brush back and forth across cheeks several times.

toothbrushes

ONE shape; palm down; move index finger back and forth across mouth several times.

triangles

Both hands ONE shape; palms out; start with index fingertips touching, then draw a triangle in the air using both index fingers; repeat.

trucks

Right hand C shape, left hand T shape; palms facing; place hands in front of chest, right hand in back of left, and move right hand staight back; repeat.

turtles

Right hand A shape, left hand C shape; right palm left, left palm down; place left hand over right hand leaving right thumb sticking out, then move thumb up and down several times.